A Special Salute to The United States Air Force

THE REAL HEROES

F-16's of the 363d Tactical Fighter Wing.

Photography by Randy Jolly

The Real Heroes is dedicated to the men and women of the United States Air Force, the
Air National Guard, and the Air Force Reserves that daily perform their quiet acts of
heroism, courage & commitment in the defense of freedom throughout the world.

The Real Heroes is also dedicated to those that made the ultimate sacrifice in the
Desert Storm conflict, particularly to the memory of a dear friend,
Captain Bradley R. Schuldt, USAF:

Born 5/18/63
Died 8/29/90

specialtypress
PUBLISHERS AND WHOLESALERS, INC.

◆

ISBN 0-933424-44-2
Designed by Laurie Adams
Printed in Hong Kong through Bookbuilders Ltd.
91 92 93 94 95 5 4 3 2 1

◆

Published by
Specialty Press, Publishers and Wholesalers, Inc.
P.O. Box 338, 123 North Second Street
Stillwater, MN 55082 U.S.A.
In Minnesota 612-430-2210, Toll-free 800-888-9653

Specialty Press books are also available at discounts for quantities for educational,
fundraising, premium, or sales-promotion use. For details contact the marketing
department. Please write or call for our free catalog of publications.

specialtypress
PUBLISHERS AND WHOLESALERS, INC.

Above photo, B-52G on final.
Cover photo, F-15E Strike Eagle taking off from a central Saudi Arabian airbase.

C-130 of the 463d Tactical Airlift Wing, Dyess Air Force Base, lifts off during a twilight sortie.

CONTENTS

Strategic Air Command

Tactical Air Command

Military Airlift Command

Air Force Systems Command

Air Force Special Operations Command

In addition to keeping the Lancer ready to go, it's my job to pass down to the younger people the knowledge and skill required to maintain this complex and demanding machine.

But when I consider the B-1's capabilities and all the effort that's gone into keeping it mission ready it makes me proud to know that I have an important part in the defense of our country. To me, that's why the countless hours of cold and sweat preparing the B-1 for its mission are more than worth it. The Lancer is simply the best there is.

Staff Sergeant/B-1B
Crew Chief

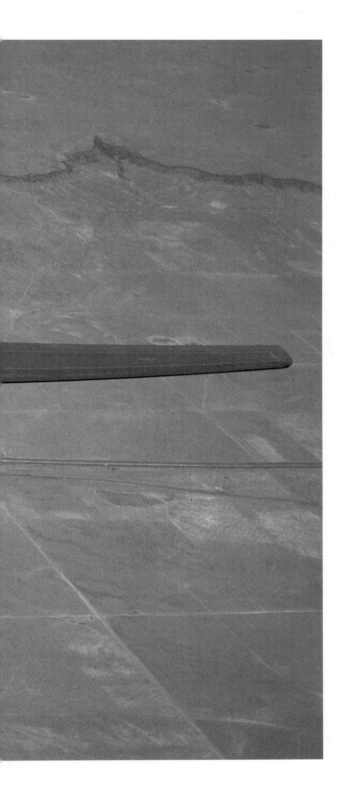

Flying the B-1B has been one of the great thrills of my life. Whenever you think of the B-1 you think speed. I can still remember my first low level in the jet. The IP had me slow to 420 knots (which, by the way, was faster than the placard in the BUFF) and then light the burners and accelerate to 600. Man, what a kick! In just a matter of seconds we were doing 600 knots and she wasn't even straining. I don't think many fighters could stay with her from 400 to 600 knots.

Another thing that comes to mind is the Lancer's agility. I had an F-16 yo-yo to convert to stern from 2 o'clock. We broke into him hard as he went up and by the time he finally converted, he was five miles in trail, out of the fight, out of ideas, and out of gas.

Lt. Colonel/Squadron Commander/B-1B

As the world's premier bomber aircraft, the B-1B packs an unequalled combination punch of speed, manueverability, payload and advanced technology.

To fly the "Bone" is to know true high performance. From takeoff roll, when her four afterburners push you back in the seat with over 120,000 pounds of thrust, until you return to base, where she easily manuevers inside smaller high performance fighter aircraft, the B-1B certainly does not disappoint.

What makes the B-1B such a formidable weapon system is its low altitude, terrain following capability. Imagine flying 200 feet above the ground going 700 miles per hour at night and in bad weather.

With a fuel capacity of over 30,000 gallons and a weapons load of 84 iron bombs or 24 nuclear weapons, no target is invulnerable to the B-1B. Such capability instills confidence and loyalty to all who fly her, and exemplifies the Air Force committment to long range strategic bombing.

1Lt./B-1B Pilot

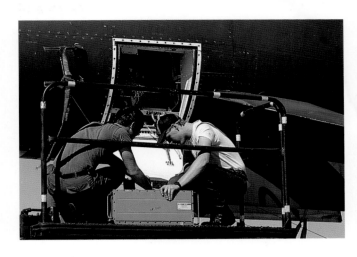

The KC-135 is an aircraft with an impeccable history of service and a sparkling future. Crewmembers love flying the venerable and able "Water Wagon" or "Steam Jet." She stands as a 35 year old queen of the jet-age fleet.

The KC-135 remains as one of the last jets designed with a slide rule and pure instinct. The controls are manual, with cables moving balance

panels which in turn move the control surfaces. The aircraft is a delight to fly. Redundancy in hydraulic systems and control surfaces

have brought this airplane and its crews back safely after tens of thousands of missions. Though the A models are underpowered by modern standards, the R model with its computer avionics, wing reskin and CFM-56 engines (which almost double the thrust) should increase the capabilities and extend the life of the KC-135 well into the 21st century.

The fact that I can imagine my children flying the KC-135 someday is a testimony to the designer's genius and the future importance of the tanker air refueling mission. I am proud to have flown an aircraft with such a brilliant history and superb flying capabilities.

Captain/KC-135 pilot

Any boom operator will tell you he has the best enlisted flying job in the world. The work really starts when the receiver says he has to make the first contact or he's "bingo fuel" (only enough fuel to reach an adequate landing base).

The ultimate challenge to a boomer is a dark night, in turbulence with an inexperienced pilot — all at the same time!

MSgt./KC-135 Boom Operator

Top: Air National Guard KC-135E refueling an F-16A. Bottom (from left): B-1B, B-52, F-15's, and F-117A.

While the KC-135's primary mission is refueling long-range strategic bombers, the -135 supports every U.S. Air Force major command that flies air refuelable aircraft as well as the U.S. Navy, and our allies.

Above and right: Equipped with a special drogue adapter, the KC-135 refuels an F/A-18 and F-14 from the USS America over the Red Sea during DESERT STORM. Below: Refueling an A-7 of the Iowa Air National Guard.

The KC-135 is an old yet extremely reliable aircraft. With over 5500 hours in the -135 I have only experienced 1 engine fire and 2 other engines shut down in flight. It's an incredibly safe airplane!

As a force multiplier, the KC-135 has no equal. The aircraft are so well maintained that they are as reliable today as when they first went into commission.

The refueling mission is as critical and demanding as any other in the air. And the crew, whose dedication and valor far outweigh the common sense one would apply when considering the implications of entering hostilities while sitting on a fuel tank, are as competent as their team bretheren. Is the KC-135 still a viable weapon system? You bet! Now, if we only had a nose gun . . . .

Major/KC-135 Navigator

Facing Page: KC-135 cockpit crew at work: pilot, co-pilot and navigator. Above: KC-135A of the 2nd Bombardment Wing on final. Left: Boom operator reviewing call signs prior to meeting up with receivers.

Who would have thought that 30 years after the first KC-135 rolled out of the Boeing plant that the Air Force would still be utilizing the same airframes? For those of us who maintain these airplanes on an everyday basis, it isn't hard to understand that the airplane is supposed to remain in the inventory till the year 2025.

But for an airplane of its size, complexity and age, there isn't a better flying airframe anywhere. I have witnessed a two week tanker task force from the States to Hawaii, to Guam, to Okinawa, back to Guam, to Hawaii, and back to the States with only one write-up. On another occasion we did a cross-country to the Mideast and back with no write-ups!

All KC-135 crew chiefs and maintenance personnel would agree that this airframe is the safest, most durable, and most versatile in the world. Fighter guys may get all the glory — but after most sorties, the tanker guys recover, refuel and button down the airplane and go home while the fighter guys are still working to get their airplanes ready for the next day.

SSgt./KC-135 Crew Chief

If you believe in destiny, then it was a plan somewhere that I worked on B-52's. The day I was born, the movie "Bombers B-52" was showing in my parent's hometown movie theatre. Trivial information — but an odd coincidence!

Being water burners, the B-52 is smoky, noisy . . . and a lot of hard work. There is, however, a certain feeling of pride in working on an airplane that others might think is less glamorous.

In my position as maintenance supervisor, I have people working in all kinds of weather, usually wet from sweat or freezing rain. I can't help but be impressed with their dedication and spirit. In my opinion, they certainly don't receive enough pay for what they are doing, but they perform anyway — out of pride and an uncommon sense of duty.

That's the reason I stay in the Air Force; the challenge of doing a good job with good people. And, the privilege of defending our country!

Captain/B-52 Maintenance Supervisor

Facing Page: B-52 H's of the 7th Bombardment Wing on Bomber Row. Above: B-52G of the 2nd Bombardment Wing undergoing routine maintenance on the flight line.

Able to carry a wide assortment of ordnance and perform a variety of missions, the B-52 continues to be the primary manned strategic bomber for the Air Force.

Top: Six AGM-86 air launch cruise missiles being loaded aboard a B-52H.
Bottom left: Rotary mounted AGM-69 SRAM missiles.
Bottom right: Mk-82 iron bombs.

Have you ever stared at the sky and at the clouds and wondered: what would it be like to take off like Superman and soar through the air? I think it was that fantasy that consciously (or subconsciously) led me to select the profession of aviation.

Of course flying is an inherently dangerous thing (afterall, if God had meant us to fly He'd have given us wings), but the thrill of "flying your aircraft through the footless halls of air" is well worth the risk.

Although flying is fun, it takes hours of intense study and literally years of in-flight experience to achieve the status of "pilot," but the exhilaration of flight is fantastic. You feel one with nature; a part of the sky. While flying at night, you feel a sense of awe as God's beautiful stars shoot across the sky. And there is nothing quite like the sunrise at 30,000 feet!

I am proud to be a military aviator. I fly the skies to keep them safe for our families and friends. Sometimes we have to do things that are necessary for the safety and security of the skies. These actions may detract from the beauty of flight, but in this day and age, we need good aviators who can enforce the laws that govern the lovely skies which look down on us.

As aviators, we will always appreciate the opportunity to dance among the clouds and "touch the face of God."

Captain/B-52 pilot

When people see the B-52 close up they often comment on how big and ugly it is. But to me, working on the -52 every day, there's a feeling of pride in being able to work on a piece of history. Although the B-52 has a rapidly aging airframe, it has constantly been updated with the most advanced avionics systems available.

It might be ugly . . . but it sure is dependable. So dependable, in fact, that the B-52 is one of the most important deterrents in the U.S. arsenal.

TSgt./B-52 Crew Chief

The KC-10 has redefined the meaning of the word capability. It employs the thrust of six F-16's, one and a half times the range of the B-52, more maximum load than the C-5, three times the fuel capacity of the KC-135, the technology of the B-1 ... and the comfort and grace of the 747. In short, the KC-10 can reliably support any aircraft, on any mission, in any command, in any service, at any location around the world.

Captain/KC-10 pilot

The KC-10 performs "advertised" as a force multiplier in that, while carrying cargo and fuel, it can refuel a wide variety of receivers.

The flight crew of a KC-10 at work: aircraft commander and pilot and engineer in the cockpit and, in the back, the boom operator works with the receivers.

At an airstrip near the Kuwaiti border a KC-10 crew chief takes personal charge of refueling his aircraft.

In the predawn hours at an eastern Saudi Arabian airfield, pallets of material are quickly off-loaded and trucked from the scene by Air Force personnel.

Few duties in any service place personnel in a more direct position to influence deterrence. We are on the front lines of strategic nuclear deterrence; every hour of every day. Deterrence can only work if the adversary or potential adversary is convinced that we are able and willing to employ our weapons effectively against him. Our training gives every Missile Launch Officer the ability and our calling as officers assures our willingness to obey lawful orders.

I enjoy my job as a Missile Launch Officer and look for- ward to the challenges that are ahead. My concern is not with the political ramifica- tions of our changing world. My responsibility, indeed my duty, is to be ultimately con- cerned with our nation's strategic position in the world and its defensive posture as directed by our civilian leaders. At times it is a thank- less job. Yet in the end, our thanks comes in the form of peace. The hard part is keep- ing this conclusion in mind during long, lonely alerts when the only threat seems to be boredom. My own thanks comes by simply knowing an

entire world can go on exist- ing because the weapons I control are not used.

The concept of deterrence and peace through strength is proven and cemented as fact each day as my ability and willingness to employ the world's most powerful and destructive weapons is not tested by an adversary. Any adversary knows that if tested, the United States is able and willing. Missiliers make sure of that. We sol- emnly make that promise and pray we're never called upon to keep it.

Lt./Deputy Missile Combat Crew Commander

From a maintenance standpoint, the conversion to the F-16 was like a breath of fresh air. And, like it or not, we were dragged into the computer age.

The F-16 continues to be highly dependable. The lower maintenance-per-flying-hour quality sometimes makes the maintenance man feel like the Maytag repairman. But there is always something to do in making the aircraft ready for the next sortie whether it's scheduled inspections or just keeping the aircraft clean.

The personal highlight of any crew chief's career is to ride back seat on a training sortie. To actually experience the end result of the diverse maintenance skills makes the job worthwhile. Be warned, however, that after a ride in the F-16 you can never again be impressed with ANY roller coaster.

MSgt./F-16 Crew Chief

The best way to describe flying the F-16 is to compare it to driving a Maserati. When they designed the F-16 they started with the pilot and built a fighter around him. The F-16 offers maximum maneuverability, weapons delivery, computer integration and superb visibility. It's so smooth and responsive you almost forget you are strapped into the jet.

When you are done flying for the day and someone sees you in your flight suit and asks "what do you fly?", all you have to say is "I fly the Viper" — that says it all.

Captain/F-16 pilot

SSGT L SMITH
SRA M WRIGHT

RESCUE

F-16's of the 64th Aggressor Squadron, subordinate unit of the 57th Fighter Weapons Wing, Nellis AFB, Nevada are an integral part of the Red Flag exercises. The F-16 aircraft are camouflaged in patterns known to be in use by potential adversaries flying Soviet-built aircraft worldwide and the pilots are uniquely trained to present what is known of Soviet fighter concepts and capabilities. The Aggressor's purpose is to create the most realistic combat training environment possible and train their opponents, operational fighter aircrews, to win!

South Carolina's Air National Guard 157th Tactical Fighter Squadron (reigning "Gunsmoke" World Champions) was part of the 4th Tactical Fighter Wing (Provisional) during DESERT STORM. Based in central Saudi Arabia, the 157th carried a wide assortment of ordnance into combat.

Excerpts from a letter written during DESERT STORM:

". . . we are sitting here in our tent with a raging sandstorm going outside. Flying has been cancelled for this morning for target weather and the fact that you can't see thirty feet in front of your face, much less breathe out there. The wind is blowing so hard that the floor of our tent is puffed up like a balloon and we even have a double layer of sandbags around the tent! The war has settled into pretty much routine for all of us now. I have about twenty to twenty-five combat sorties personally and 2,000 hours in the first thirty days of the war.

There are plenty of targets still to hit though! We have been pounding the Republican Guards on an almost daily basis for the last two weeks. Yesterday we went about ninety miles south of Baghdad and hit some artillery and anti-aircraft positions. That was our farthest penetration north thus far. We sent six ships and I was leading the last element. By the time we got to the target area the AAA had been taken out so I rolled in on a big revetted compound full of vehicles and got a huge secondary out of my bombs!"

Lt. Colonel/pilot F-16

Right: "Cobra" marking unique to the 174th's F-16's. *Middle:* Showing off its ability to carry a wide assortment of ordnance, F-16's with CBU (cluster) munitions and MK-82 500 lb. iron bombs.

Facing page: An F-16 of the 174th Tactical Fighter Wing, New York Air National Guard ("The Boys from Syracuse"), touches down at an airbase in central Saudi Arabia. During DESERT STORM, 174th was part of the 4th Tactical Fighter Wing (Provisional).

Climbing into an F-16 is like putting on a glove. The airplane was designed around the pilot. Once set up on the ground the pilot never has to go heads down to find a switch. Almost anything can be accessed through the Up Front Control conveniently located directly in front of the pilot just below the HUD. The pilot can drop a bomb, come off target, get a radar lock on a bandit and shoot the bandit down with either a missile or the gun without ever taking his hands off the throttle or stick.

The F-16 is one of the most accurate and lethal bombers ever built when in the Air-to-Ground mode, yet all it takes is a flick of the thumb to change one switch on the throttle and it combines the small size and high maneuverability to become the best dogfighter in the world.

Captain/F-16 pilot

F-16C's of the 69th Tactical Fighter Squadron (based at Moody AFB) head for home over the Saudi Arabian desert.

The most surprising thing about the F-117 is that it looks so different from any other airplane. You can't see the fuselage from the cockpit — so when flying it feels like you are at the tip of a spear. It's very exhilarating. Even though the F-117, or black jet, is radically different in appearance — it handles much like any other fighter in the Air Force. It's a reliable and easy plane to fly and performs its mission with incredible precision.

Captain/F-117A pilot

*To the demon that seeks the
hood of the night, beware,
the one who rides the shadows
sees YOU!*

The F-117A is an excellent aircraft to fly. The best part is being a member of an elite community flying the #1 fighter in the world. The people, both officers and enlisted are the best in the Air Force.

The planes are so new (many have less than 100 hours) that they still smell new. The systems are very reliable and the F-117A hardly ever breaks.

Not only is the airplane a dream to fly, but the mission is great too. My background is with F-111's which makes the night flying mission of the F-117A easier. There is a tremendous amount of satisfaction flying the best and newest aircraft in the Air Force inventory. Both my wife and I are very proud to be part of the STEALTH family!

Captain/F-117A pilot

It's exciting to be, in my own way, a part of this extraordinary project. This is an aircraft that just a few years ago could only be dreamed of in a science fiction novel.

As far as maintenance goes, this aircraft is what F-4 crew chiefs and specialists only dream about. The F-117 was designed and built to be repaired quickly and efficiently. Not only that . . . the F-117 has a very good reliability rate.

One of the reasons I enjoy my job is the fact that only a handfull of people on the entire planet have even touched this airplane . . . and I get to work on it every day!

Ssgt/F-117A Crew Chief

Members of the 1st Tactical Fighter Wing — 94th Aircraft Maintenance Unit — perform an ICT exercise (Integrated Combat Turnaround). While simultaneously refueling and servicing the aircraft, four AIM-9 Sidewinders and four AIM-7 Sparrow air-to-air missiles are loaded along with 940 rounds of 20mm ammunition and eight modules of chaff and flare countermeasure devices. ICT training is crucial to keeping the aircraft and crews operationally ready.

Tsgt Clyde Riddle Jr
A1C Albert Burkhalte

Though often unheralded, maintenance and ground crews worked round the clock, greatly contributing to the success of the combat sorties flown during DESERT STORM. At a central Saudi Arabian airbase, maintenance crews of the 53rd Tactical Fighter Wing perform routine maintenance on two battle tested F-15C's.

For a crew chief, the F-15 is hard to beat. It is an easy plane to work on. It's a tough jet that can take a lot of punishment and keep on flying. In my opinion, there's no other aircraft like it. Keeping the world's best superiority fighter flying is a great honor.

SSgt./F-15 Crew Chief

Every time I fly the F-15, my mind gets stuck on one word . . . AWESOME! This airplane has been the premier air-to-air fighter in the world for nearly 20 years. That would be like flying a fabric and wire biplane against Mustangs and Messerschmidts in WWII . . . awesome.

Captain/F-15 pilot

Above: F-15C's in a large revetment at a central Saudi Arabian airbase.

Facing page: A Bitburg F-15C (53rd Tactical Fighter Wing), launches from its Saudi airbase during DESERT STORM. The 53rd TFW served as part of the 4th Tactical Fighter Wing (Provisional) during the conflict and scored several air-to-air "kills."

If God had said "let there be fighters," He would have been talking about the F-15. Porsche's advertising slogan a few years ago fits the Eagle perfectly: "Nothing else comes close."

The aircraft is exceptionally reliable from a safety perspective, remarkably easy to fly, and is absolutely unbeatable in the right hands. It was designed around a superb fire control systems that can locate and track targets at any altitude, at any airspeed, and at exceptionally long — or short — ranges.

Cockpit ergonomics are extremely pilot friendly and allow for a totally "heads out" operation of the fire control system to employ radar missiles, heat seeking missiles, or the gun. The bubble canopy and high sitting position afford the pilot unsurpassed, 360 degree view of the world outside and an easy "tally" on any bandit aircraft in visual range.

The F-15 is truly a fighter pilot's dream.

Lt. Colonel/F-15 pilot

Facing page: F-15's of the 21st Tactical Fighter Wing flying combat air patrol over Alaska. Top: Loading an AIM-9 Sidewinder. Middle: Taxiing out with target drogue on centerline. Bottom: Loading AIM-7 Sparrow's.

The real unsung heroes are the crew chiefs — "wrench benders" as we call them. I'll never forget the look on my crew chief's face when we brought our jet home after a high-speed, low altitude mission. He always wore a grimace when we taxied in, but this time it became worse. As we brought our once immaculate Vark closer to him, he could see just how much paint we had literally burned off the F-111's leading edges. We had even peeled back the neoprene coating on the blade antennas! He had a lot of work to do that night. Sure enough, next morning the Vark was ready to go again, looking none the worse for wear from our previous day's work — tribute to our crew chief's pride in doing a job well. Without him, we could never get wheels in the well.

Lt. Colonel, Squadron Commander/F-111

PILOT
CAPT BUSSA
CREW CHIEF
SSGT NEMETH

103

The F-111 embodies technology that was far ahead of its time. To those of us who fly the F-111, she's the Cadillac of fighter-bombers. When you get the Vark down to a few hundred feet above the ground, fold her wings back and pick the smash up to 500 knots or so, she seems as safe and stable as the old Cadillac Dad used to drive.

Of course the amazing thing is that the F-111 can perform supersonic, low altitude attack twenty-four hours a day, regardless of the weather. Ask any F-111 driver and he'll tell you that, given the choice, he would wage war during the worst possible weather, in the middle of the darkest night. It's the environment that's belonged to the F-111 for nearly a quarter of a century. We train there — we're confident there. That's not to say that my heart doesn't beat just a little faster during a night terrain following sortie, but I'm absolutely confident that my F-111 is equipped to handle the job.

Colonel/F-111 pilot

The E-3 is a very demanding aircraft to fly. Not because it's temperamental, far from it. The trusty Boeing 707 airframe is one of the most forgiving ever made. The demanding aspects of the E-3 are the complexity of its design and the rigors of its mission.

The E-3 requires that the pilot be not only a skilled aviator, but a real systems expert as well. Commanding a crew of thirty-six officers and enlisted personnel leaves little room for indecisiveness. The sophistication of the onboard electronics require constant vigilance. I can recall many many air refuelings. Refueling a large aircraft is one of the biggest challenges a pilot can face. Refueling the E-3 isn't hard, it just takes a lot of practice, concentration, and above all patience.

After the refueling, it's into the orbit, where hour after hour of endless surveillance and weapons controlling activity takes place. This is where the mission crew earns their pay . . . working the electronic magic that has made the distinctively shaped E-3 famous world-wide. For the pilots, this is where you "rack up the hours" for your logbook.

missions being saved because a highly trained and alert crew was able to diagnose and repair an inflight problem that otherwise would have meant cancelling a mission that carried national security implications.

A typical AWACS mission usually lasts from twelve to sixteen hours, with morning briefings often starting at 3 am. The fatigue factor is ever present and relentless.

Just after sunrise, and well into the mission, you prepare for what may be the first of The E-3 is not only a great airplane to fly, but it has a phenomenal mission. A vital aspect of our peacetime diplomatic strategy as well as an indispensable wartime asset, the E-3 truly is on the leading edge.

It isn't every day that a pilot can see the results of his day's work on the evening news, however for the E-3 pilot, it's a routine occurrence.

Captain/E-3 pilot

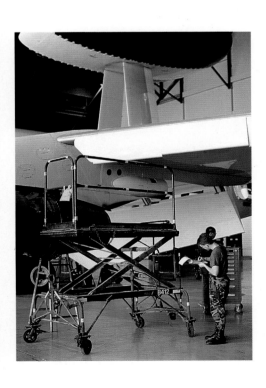

The Airborne Warning and Control System is a highly sophisticated weapon system. The foundation of the AWACS is a reliable, heavily-modified Boeing 707. The radar, computer and communications systems are the best in the world and it's maintained by dedicated air- men that go the extra mile in making sure everything works. You get a real sense of pride when you've worked all night and, because of your efforts, the mission the next day is a success.

TSgt./E-3 Maintenance Specialists

Facing Page: At a central Saudi Arabia airbase, E-3 AWAC aircraft are readied for round-the-clock missions. Right: Distinctive "skull-and-crossed bones" markings unique to E-3's in the Desert Storm conflict. Below: Security Police stands guard on E-3's just outside sand-bagged bunker.

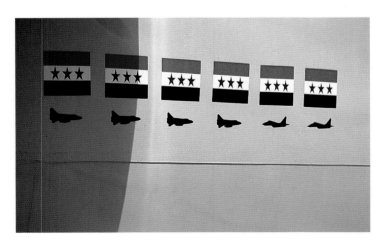

"Kill" markings painted on the side of an E-3 indicate successful air combat for allied fighters controlled by this AWACS.

To paraphrase Hemingway, men are faithful to and have a special feeling for the first fighter they fly. And so it goes with the venerable F-4. It's big, loud, ugly and dirty. But, in my opinion, the F-4 is the finest of the world's second generation fighters. I first flew the F-4 in 1972. The feeling then, and now, is of awesome power that makes me feel invincible.

Lt. Colonel/F-4 pilot

The F-4 Phantom is a real mechanic's dream. You have to troubleshoot each problem one at a time. It's not like the newer aircraft where you troubleshoot by swapping out LRU's (Line Replaceable Units). On the F-4, you have to call upon all your maintenance skills to make adjustments and solve aircraft discrepancies. You can really get into your work as there is a tremendous feeling of accomplishment after working the systems on the F-4.

The F-4 is the most durable and expandable aircraft I have ever worked on. With its ability to accept continuous upgrades and modifications, this 1960's airframe has accomplished every task and charge set upon it well into the 1990's.

MSgt./F-4 mechanic

The F-4 is like the SPAD VII, the P-51 and the F-86. It's the yardstick by which every other fighter of its generation, and those that follow, are (or will be) measured.

When I started flying the "Rhino" it was no longer the world's pre-eminent fighter aircraft. There were others that could turn tighter, bomb better, had better radars and could go farther on less fuel. Despite this, F-4's still brought home lots of gun camera film of these "better" jets and still were tough to beat in bombing competitions.

I guess what I liked best about the jet was that she made you work. She was easy to fly but tough to fly well. On a low level, a map, compass, clock and sweat got you to the target — not cosmic electrons. Until ARNY came along, it was your skill that put the bombs on the target. In air to air, you could still beat F-15s and 16s, but skill and cunning had to defeat youth and enthusiasm (and 9G turns). I'm sure the newer jets are fun to fly but there's no way they can match the satisfaction of a good sortie in the F-4.

I've got about a million and a half memories flying the F-4. The air conditioning — it simply didn't work under 10,000 feet on a warm day, which made low levels "fun."

Going supersonic down the Panamint Valley and seeing the shock waves out the side of the jet. The pleasure of flying with a good backseater and the agony of flying with a poor one (Pitters feel the same way about flying with good and weak "nose gunners"). The way the jet would rock slightly, side to side, as you rippled off bombs. The lousy visibility out the front of the jet. The lousy visibility out the back of the jet. The exhilaration of a burner climb. The feel of the jet at 540 knots and 100 feet — solid as a rock but still very maneuverable (unless you were heavy . . . then just solid as a rock). The sweet taste of watching your opponent screw up in air to air and knowing that you "have" him. The frustration and anger of screwing up in air to air and knowing your opponent "has" you.

Hemingway wrote a little paragraph on flying fighters that's pretty well known by those of us that do. It basically starts out that if the first fighter you fly is a great airplane, "then there your heart will always be." I may go on to fly other jets . . . but my heart will always be with the F-4!

Major/F-4 pilot

Airplanes fly like they look, and the OV-10 is no exception. The OV is unique, starting when you taxi out using the props for directional control instead of the nose wheel steering. This takes some getting used to. You sit in this huge cockpit with the canopy coming down around your knees and it feels like you're sitting on the end of a diving board. All that cockpit comes in handy since FAC's carry their weight in maps. And all that plexiglass is the perfect grease pencil notepad! Although the airplane can turn up its own rearend, it's kinda heavy on the controls.

The view is fabulous, except at 6 o'clock — where it needs to be good, of course, but is really horrible. The Air Force flies the OV-10 single pilot. So there you are, in the weeds, trying not to get lost or stray into some artillery live fire area, five radios blaring simultaneously and everybody needs to talk to you *now.* You try to plot the run-in for the fighters from IP to target with a map in your lap, the Army is screaming for "air" NOW (to save their ---) and the fighters just called saying their gas is running low. Oh, yeah, and the weather is at minimums. . . .

The OV has this wonderful habit of wallowing around in turbulence, which makes instrument flying in bumpy weather a "special" experience. In icing, the props throw ice on to the back canopy. The resulting sound can be described as an explosion. The first time it happened to me was at night after about an hour of quiet (for an OV) flying. From half-asleep to "Yo, glands, keep that adrenaline coming," I was sure the airplane was coming unglued.

It'll never be called pretty, and it could really use another 1000 hp, but for Forward Air Control you can't beat the OV.

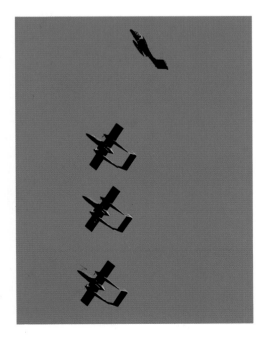

It's got good legs (loiter capability), is reasonably fast (200 Kts) and maneuverable. And the view is unreal!

Although light bombs can be carried by the OV, our primary ordnance is the 2.75" rocket with a phosphorous warhead for marking targets.

Since the altitude, airspeed and dive angle have to be just right, TLAR (That Looks About Right) is the FAC's favored delivery method. We have guys in the squadron who, when the bulb burns out in their sight, use a grease pencil mark on the sight to aim with. They often do as well as pilots with working sights.

A good OV will cruise around 180 knots which isn't too bad but the plane has zero "excess thrust" — lose an engine below 110 knots and you're about to be an ejection seat test pilot!

Major/OV-10 pilot

The EF-111A "Spark Vark" or "Raven" as it is officially called, has a little known history within the United States Air Force and an often misunderstood mission. In the early 70's forty two F-111A's were converted into the Air Force's most modern jamming platform. In spite of the modifications, we retained the ability to cruise up to 1800 nautical miles unrefueled at high altitude, to go supersonic at 100 feet and to operate at night or in the worst weather due to our terrain following radar. In addition to these capabilities, the conversion gave us the means to jam a wide spectrum of radar systems.

Being a limited asset, we are "the few ... the most sought after." Since its inception, the Raven has

The EF-111A Raven is able to consistently perform its missions — from Arctic cold to Arabian heat — because of the superior skills and dedication of our maintenance force . . . The Raven Keepers! This team of experts works around the clock to keep our aircraft flying. In terms of effort, one hour of flying takes up to thirty-five hours of maintenance work.

While the complex electronics and flight control systems of the EF-111 are the hardest to maintain, they provide the U.S. with the Raven edge in a conflict anywhere . . . anytime.

Lt. Colonel/EF-111 Squadron Commander

been designed as an offensive weapon. We were called upon in support of the Libyan raid (Eldorado Canyon), the liberation of Panama (Just Cause), and now the halting of naked aggression against defenseless Kuwait (Operation Desert Storm). Due to our constant and realistic training, we have been extremely successful in our missions throughout the world. Most of the aircrews flying the EF-111 are captains on their second tour, bringing a great deal of skill and ability to our outfits. As electronic warriors, our job is to turn every airplane in the combat package into a stealth aircraft . . . to blind the adversary's eyes by disrupting his radar. Due to the nature of our mission, we are the first to enter a hostile environment and the last to leave.

"Check Six"
We have Twelve covered.

The F-15E Strike Eagle is the leading edge of the new generation fighter aircraft. I've worked on older aircraft such as the F-4E and have a tremendous amount of respect for the "Rhino," but in today's maintenance field, the F-15E is the elite crew chief's fighter.

There's no question in my mind that the F-15E is the ultimate fighter in this day and age.

Sgt./F-15E Crew Chief

In the Saudi desert, ground crews prepare F-15E Strike Eagles of the 4th Tactical Fighter Wing for combat patrols. The tremendously high mission rate, tons of ordnance dropped, and the number of scud sites and tanks killed is a tribute to the skill and daring of the aircrews and the hard work, under extreme conditions, performed by the ground crews.

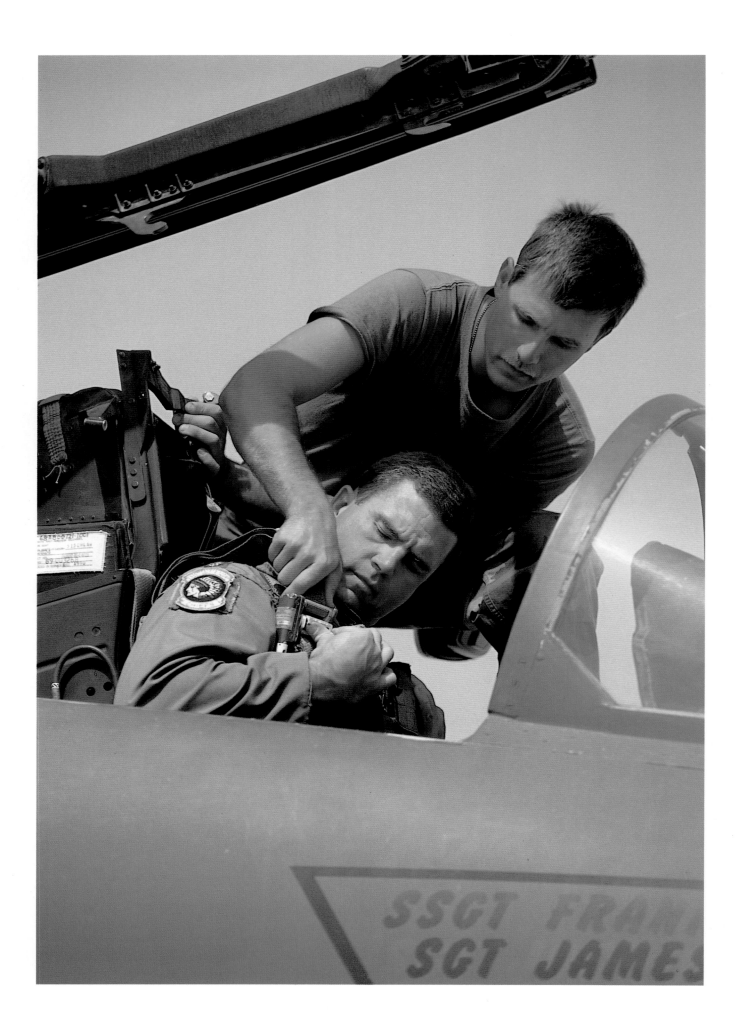

While the pilot finishes up the paper work, the WSO (weapon systems officer) gives his F-15E the once over minutes before take off.

Teamwork! Facing page: At an airbase in central Saudi Arabia, a Crew Chief of the 4th Tactical Fighter wing assists his pilot prior to a combat air patrol mission.

Excerpts from a letter received during the war with Iraq.

"We dropped some of the first bombs of the war. We took 24 jets in at low altitude against five targets in North-western Iraq. Our targets were Scud missiles. They never knew we were coming. I dropped on an airfield which had its runway lights on! However, once my bombs hit all hell broke loose. Lots of flak and SAMS (ballistically fired). On the way out two Migs ran on us ... but both crashed trying to convert to our "six." The good news was we *all* made it home.

Since then we have flown over 800 sorties, 2400 hours and dropped 5 million pounds of bombs. Today we divide our time between Scud hunting and tank killing in Kuwait.

The F-15E has proven to be an exceptional aircraft and more than met every challenge."

Lt. Colonel/Squadron Commander
F-15E pilot

The F-15E is the most impressive fighter in the world today. Every time I fly, I'm in awe of its incredible power. Climbing straight up to nearly 3 miles above the ground just after takeoff is one example of the brute force of the Eagle. Despite its raw power, it handles like a dream. Combining the two creates a very lethal weapons system that can pull 9 Gs and kill any adversary in the air today. It's the LANTIRN System that gives this plane the edge, however. It turns night into day, allowing me to fly as low as I please, even on the darkest night. All of these capabilities allow the WSO and me to deliver bombs on target anytime, anywhere.

1st Lt./F-15E pilot

The A-10 is rugged and reliable, easy to fly — but demanding to employ tactically. It is perfectly suited for the mission of close air support. With its 30 mm gatling gun it is probably the best airframe for low intensity conflict ever designed. New modifications make it as accurate as more modern aircraft with computer delivery systems.

"Hog" drivers are a proud breed. We are determined and prepared to perform a tough job well.

Captain/A-10 pilot

Being a dedicated crew chief on the A-10, "Thunderbolt II" puts you in a class by yourself. Just the thought of a weapon system that powerful is awesome.

I guess the A-10 is not as glamorous or attention getting as some of its counterparts, but I can honestly say it is one of the most reliable and maintainable aircraft in the Air Force. Granted, it is probably the ugliest aircraft I know of, which is why we call it the "Warthog." But appearances can be deceiving! The best way I can describe the A-10 is to say it is a dynamic package of power and performance. One of the gratifying aspects of my job is watching the most effective and devastating air-to-ground aircraft in the United States Air Force lift off on a mission, knowing it has been maintained by the few, the proud — the "Hog Keepers"!!!

Sgt./A-10 Dedicated Crew Chief

I've accumulated over 2,000 hours in the A-7 and have come to admire its special qualities. It's not a particularly pretty airplane or strikingly beautiful, but its virtues include strength, dependability and stamina. Above all, it is a precision weapons delivery system. Having witnessed this accuracy many times from the A-7 cockpit, I've often thought how I would dislike being on the receiving end of its bombing and strafing attacks.

Lt. Colonel/A-7D pilot

The A-7 is the first plane I ever turned a bolt on and it continues to be a very simple and easy system to maintain in spite of the numerous modifications and very complex capabilities.

It may not be fast. It certainly isn't pretty compared to the more modern fighters — but its record for carrying lots of ordnance and putting it precisely on target speaks for itself.

MSgt./A-7 Crew Chief

When it's cold, she's cold. When it's hot, she's hot. When she's good . . . she's very good!! And when troops or equipment or material need to get to the front, the C-130 can be counted on to do the job.

From the maintenance standpoint, this is one of the most rewarding aircraft in the Air Force to work on. You can see how your efforts directly relate to the mission, and you feel an exhilarating sense of pride when your aircraft taxis out, takes the runway, and then takes off.

MSgt./C-130 Crew Chief

Among the many roles filled by the C-130, none is more important than the quick movement of the wounded and injured from the front lines. At a Saudi Arabian airbase, C-130's and C-141's prepare for flights to medical facilities in Europe and the States.

Facing Page: First stop on the way home. Troops flown from a forward air base in Saudi Arabia aboard an Air National Guard C-130 make the first stop prior to the long haul home. Below: Whether it's carrying troops — or material in their support — the C-130 is always on the job.

She was there for Vietnam . . . She was there for Grenada . . . She was there for Panama . . . and, she was there for Desert Storm!

During any contingency, disaster relief support, humanitarian effort, peacetime strategic airlift, combat airlift of troops, aeromedical evacuation of the wounded or special operations at low level, the work horse of airlift — the C-141 Starlifter — has seen it all.

Since her birth in 1961, the C-141 has been underestimated. We've stretched her 23 feet to maximize her airlift capabilities, installed a refueling port and asked her to do low level operations for us. Impressively, she's accomplished it all with one of the best safety records in the Air

Force. She was the backbone of Viet Nam airlift, is a veteran of numerous humanitarian relief efforts, and has hauled everything from machines of war, to whales for Sea World, to lettuce and tomatoes. Her crews must be as diversified as she. They are tasked to fly missions entailing everything from air refueling, to airdrop at McMurdo Research Station in the Antarctic, to combat airdrop missions over Panama.

Mostly unknown, basically unglamorous, she does her job in the dark alleys of the world. The C-141 is definitely a key to our national security . . . definitely a plane I am proud to fly!

Lt./C-141 Navigator

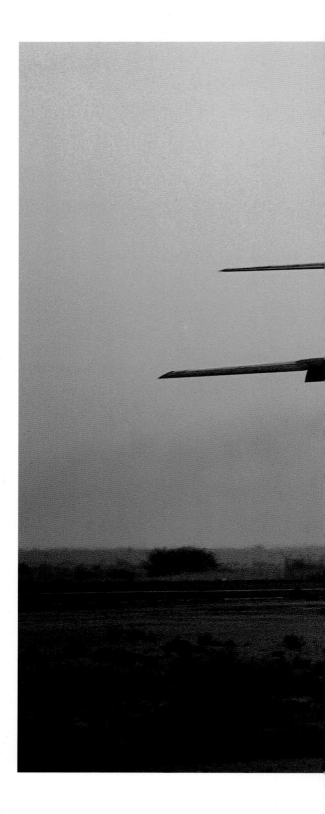

*Previous and following page:
Around the clock flights by
C-141's to an airstrip in eastern
Saudi Arabia provide a constant
supply of troops and material.*

A C-141 on final at an airstrip
in eastern Saudi Arabia.

Whether it's in support of the 82nd Airborne or bringing equipment and material to the front, the -141 has proven to be a reliable workhorse of the Military Airlift Command.

The C-5 is an awesome airplane in every respect. Its sheer size and airlift capability amaze me everytime I fly it. It's a pilot's airplane; very forgiving and fun to fly. I can't think of a better airplane to fly around the world in.

Captain/C-5 pilot

The C-5's capabilities have to be seen to be understood. After working on the C-5 for nine years and flying on it for five, I have come to appreciate and respect this huge flying machine.

The C-5 is one of the few aircraft in today's Air Force where the mechanic is allowed to fly. This opportunity allows maintenance people to work on the aircraft and experience the missions first hand.

That aircraft has so many systems that are unique. My job is to keep the systems going so the mission can continue uninterrupted. When flying, this means working long days — sometimes 20 hours or more.

But there is no greater feeling than the satisfaction that comes from knowing that you alone repaired a malfunction that enabled the aircraft to take off and complete its mission. It's hard to describe the excitement of sitting behind the pilot during a maximum gross weight take-off, knowing that you will use up every foot of runway to get the airplane airborne.

You will never see, today, an aircraft that is more dependable than the C-5 or one that can move such huge amounts of troops and equipment. If you ask me, the C-5 puts the "backbone" in MAC's motto "The Backbone of Deterrence."

Staff Sergeant/C-5 Crew Chief

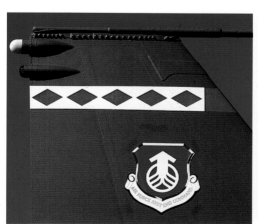

The F-l5E Strike Eagle is truly one of aviation's great fighters. It was built to combine the most advanced technology for its dual role of air-to-air and air-to-ground and drops about five times the bombload of other jets on the line. Inside the cockpt it is truly cosmic!

I feel extremely lucky to be a test pilot on this aircraft.

The Eagle has lived up to its name, has proven itself in combat, and will continue to be the best aircraft in the world.

Captain/F-l5E Test Pilot

The F-4 is a mean looking airplane meant to do one thing . . . go to war. The newer aircraft can take the Phantom's place in the inventory but will have a long haul before thay can match its hard won reputation in combat.

In our work, the Phantom is a rock solid jet. It can virtually do everything; high speed chase, ordnance test and carry anything in the inventory. Because of it's versatility, the F-4 is an excellent evaluation and systems integration platform.

Lt. Colonel/F-4 Weapons Systems Officer

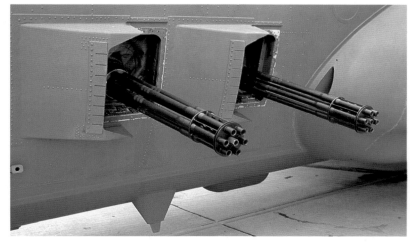

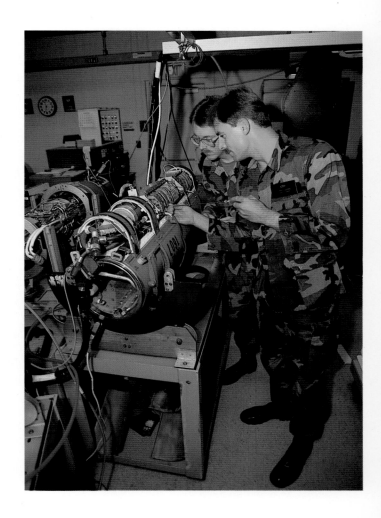

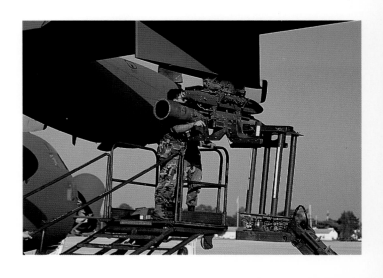

The 16th Special Operations Squadron is one of five special operations squadrons of the 1st Special Operations Wing. Flying the AC-130H "Spectre" gunship, the 16th SOS flies close air support, armed reconnaissance, interdiction, night search and rescue, and airborne command and control missions.

Equipped with infrared and low-light television detection systems and sensors and a computertized fire control system, the Spectre is a formidable flying arsenal. Armament includes two 20mm Vulcan cannons that each fire 2,500 rounds a minute, a 40mm Bofors cannon firing 100 rounds a minute, and a specially modified Army Howitzer that fires up to four rounds a minute.

Facing page: AC-130H Spectre gunship firing flares. Right: Firing the 105mm Army Howitzer.

The 20th Special Operations Squadron, Green Hornets, flies the MH-53J Pave Low helicopter.

The 20th SOS's primary mission is to conduct day or night low level penetration into hostile territory to accomplish clandestine infiltration/exfiltration and aerial gunnery support.

The MH-53J is distinguishable from other versions of the -53 by its retractable air refueling probe, external hoist, two jettisonable auxiliary fuel tanks, armor plating and 7.62mm and .50 caliber machine guns.

With the aid of night vision goggles (NVG), Pave Low crews carry out their missions in the darkest night to arrive over target undetected.

The MH-53J is one of the most sophisticated helicopters in the world. With its terrain following/terrain avoidance/ground mapping radar, mission computer, FLIR (forward looking infrared receiver), Doppler/inertial navigation and electronic counter-measure system, the MH-53J is well suited for its very unique mission.

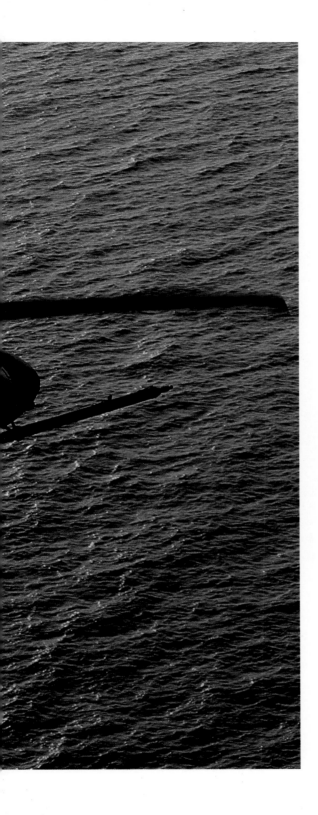

The 55th Special Operations Squadron, flying the MH-60G, flies long-range, low-level, communications-out, night penetration missions into hostile territory.

The MH-60G Pave Hawk is perfectly suited for the job. With air refueling capabilities, extensive navigation and communication equipment along with defensive fire power, the MH-60Gs of the 55th SOS and its NVG equipped crews perform special operations and combat rescue missions for U.S. and allied special forces.

The REAL HEROES would not have been possible without the heroic efforts of hundreds of men and women at every level within the Air Force. Hopefully, the images in this book will be a token of my thanks to everyone's hard work and long suffering.

Special thanks, however, goes to Lt. Colonel Don Black for his insight, constant encouragement — and friendship. Thanks also to Brigadier General Ed Robertson, Lt. Colonel James Ragan, Colonel Ron Sconyers, Colonel Larry Greer, Colonel Hal Hornburg, Colonel Vic Andrews, Colonel Bill McAdams and Lt. Colonels "Steep" Turner and "Slammer" Decuir. Many thanks also to Major Dave Mason, Major Janet Tucker, Major Gordy Larson, Captain Steve Solmonson, Captain Kevin Baggett, Captain Dave Turner, Captain Julie Holland, Lt. Cathy Reardon, MSgt. Steve Pivnick and TSgt. Ike Isaacson.

Hundreds of others worked night and day to make things happen; life support for patiently suiting me up for flight, pilots that have endured straight and level flight, ground crews and maintenance personnel that have worked after hours to help get those "special" photo opportunities and the Security Police for being lenient even when I accidentally stepped over red lines!

To each and everyone, THE REAL HEROES is a tribute to your friendship, kindness and professionalism.

Photo credits: All photos by the author with the following exceptions — Major Many Montejano (F-111's from Lackenheath) and TSgt. Ike Isaacson (C-141 in flight).